MUKLUKS FOR
Annabelle

Based on the true story of Annabelle,
the baby elephant at the Alaska Zoo

Written and illustrated by Dianne Barske

PC PUBLICATION
CONSULTANTS
PUBLISHING THE WORKS OF AUTHORS WORLDWIDE
Because We Believe In The Power Of Authors

PO Box 221974 Anchorage, Alaska 99522-1974
books@publicationconsultants.com—www.publicationconsultants.com

ISBN 978-1-63747-023-7

Library of Congress Catalog Card Number 2021936578

© 2021 Dianne Barske

—Third Edition—

First Edition, August 1999

Second Printing, August 2004

Manufactured in the United States of America.

Dedication

This simple story is dedicated to Sammye Seawell, without whom there would be no Alaska Zoo and there would have been no Annabelle to win the hearts of Anchorage.

How It All Began

Mukluks for Annabelle is based on a true story. Sammye Seawwell, director of the Alaska Zoo, brought the baby elephant named Annabelle to her horse barn on the Anchorage hillside in 1966. She had seen the little elephant, kept in a grocery store parking lot on a chain. The elephant had been won in a national contest sponsored by Chiffon Tissue. The contest winner was offered $3000 or an elephant. The Anchorage winner, obviously with a fine-tuned sense of humor, chose the elephant!

Sammye explains, "At the time of the story, the little elephant was in my care and there was no zoo. The zoo evolved from so many people coming to see the elephant and my need for a place to keep her where people could see her."

As the weather grew colder, it became apparent that a solution must be found for the baby elephant's feet in the snow and cold, or Annabelle would have to be confined to her barn. "I took her walking every day, and I knew I was going to have to address her need for foot gear," Sammye said.

Sammye made everything in the line of elephant foot-wear she could think of – from hand-knitted socks to felt booties. "Nothing worked," she remembers with a sigh.

Anchorage may have cold winters, but the community often displays a warm heart. "People jumped in to help. They brought me everything," Sammye recalls. "You wouldn't believe all the knitted things, crocheted things, things out of felt – all kinds of booties. It was quite a collection."

Finally, Alaskan ingenuity and know-how prevailed. What had worked so well for Alaska's Native people for centuries could work for this new little four-footed import – mukluks – Native made-boots sewn from seal skin or moose hide, and designed to provide snug, air-tight warmth in the coldest weather.

And so four elephant mukluks came into being – large enough to accommodate baby elephant feet – mukluks for Annabelle, the little elephant that won the heart of her new home, Anchorage, Alaska.

Annabelle, the baby elephant, peeked out of her barn door. It was cold and white outside the barn.

Big snowflakes were falling.

The children at the winter zoo watched her.

"Why does she stay in her barn?" one little girl wondered out loud.

She tugged at her grandmother's sleeve.

"Why does she only put her trunk outside?

Why?"

She could remember springtime when the elephant,
even smaller then, would come out to play with her
and the other children. Sometimes the baby elephant
would chase after the squirrels and ravens.

"Why doesn't she come out into the snow and chase snowflakes?"

"Why?"

"Why?" her grandmother repeated.

"Alaska is a strange and different place for a baby elephant, especially in our winter. Elephants are not used to snowflakes. Elephants are used to warm grass and warm feet, not cold feet in the snow."

Annabelle watched the white world outside. She saw two children, sledding on a snow-covered hill. This world was her new home, Alaska. She had been brought north to Anchorage and would one day live in the Alaska Zoo. She'd left her warm, familiar world far behind.

Annabelle stuck her trunk out the door, catching snowflakes on it. Then she stretched her trunk out further into the cold and thumped it on the wooden sides of her barn.

THUMP!
THUMP!

The little girl listened and watched, silently now, beside her grandmother. Her name was Qalu, an Eskimo name. She was from far north Alaska, Barrow or Utqiagvik, and was visiting her grandmother in Anchorage.

Qalu began to sway her arms side-to-side, copying the swinging of the baby elephant's trunk. She thumped her boots in the snow.

THUMP!

THUMP!

She made deep footprints.

"Aaka, Grandma, the elephant wants to come out," she said finally, tugging on the sleeve of Grandma's parka. Aaka is her Eskimo word for grandmother.

15

"She doesn't understand snow and winter," Grandma replied softly. She, too, watched Annabelle, moving only her trunk, keeping her feet well inside her barn's doorway. "She wants to come out, but her feet hurt in the cold."

Qalu looked down at her own warm feet. She loved to let her feet go stomping and tromping out in the snow, making a trail. "Mukluks," she whispered, just loud enough for her grandmother to hear.

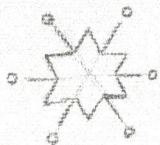

"Mukluks!"

she said much louder.

"Yes!" her grandmother nodded, understanding what Qalu was telling her.

"It is your mukluks - your winter boots - that let you thump and jump and play in the snow," she told Qalu.

"It is the mukluks I made for you that keep your feet warm in winter's cold. I could make mukluks for Annabelle."

Qalu smiled. That was what she was trying to tell Grandma. She knew her grandmother could do it. She could make mukluks for Annabelle. She'd made many pairs of mukluks for Qalu and for other children so they could play in the snow.

Grandma got her sewing things.

She got brown paper to trace Annabelle's feet.
This time she needed bigger brown paper for
elephant feet. Grandma got some moose hide
for the bottoms of Annabelle's mukluks.

Grandma's needle went back and
forth, in and out, double stitching
she called it – for strength. She
used caribou hide for the tops and
then put holes in it and made strips
of caribou for leather lacings.

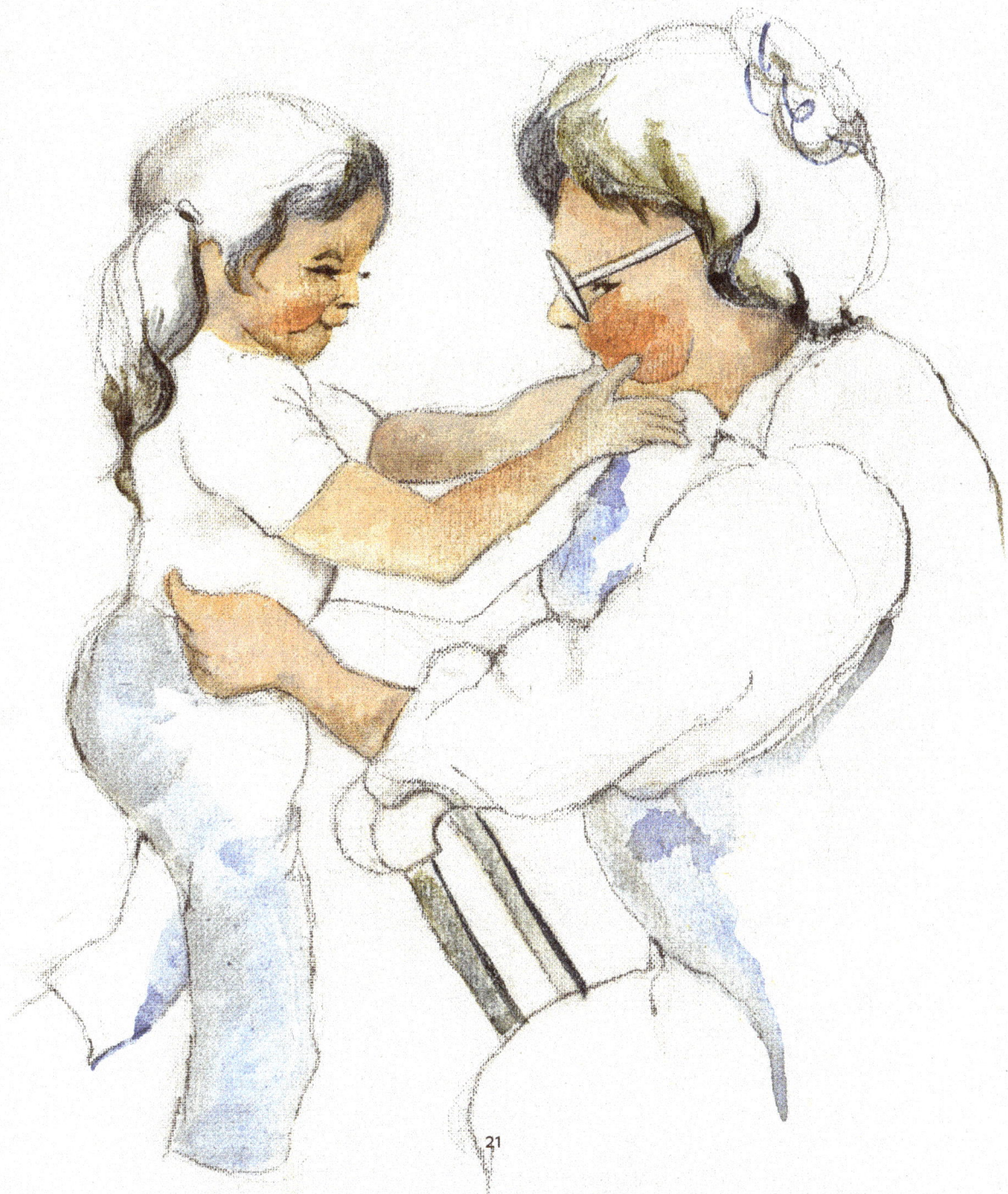

She was done – four mukluks for Annabelle.

Grandma and Qalu shared a happy hug.

Grandma and Qalu watched as Annabelle first wore her mukluks. For a few minutes, she stayed in the barn door.

Back and forth, back and forth, she was swinging her trunk, still keeping her feet in their new mukluks inside the door. The snow – white and cold and deeper now – was still new to Annabelle.

Then she put one foot into the snow, then another, then all four feet. She stomped, and small puffs of new snow flew into the cold air. She felt around in the snow with her trunk. Here was something new! Someone had built her a snowman friend!

Grandma smiled. She was proud of her mukluks. "Her feet are warm now and do not hurt," she said.

Qalu grinned, too, watching the baby elephant
take her first stomping steps in the snow.

She held her grandmother's
hand. Snowflakes fell gently,
all around. Annabelle left
big, deep footprints, like
white pockets, in the snow.

Four elephant feet were
warm and snug in the
mukluks for Annabelle.

www.ingramcontent.com/pod-product-compliance
Lightning Source LLC
LaVergne TN
LVHW070836080426
835509LV00027B/3489